DOODLES
AND HAPPY THOUGHTS

ELIZABETH D'ANDREA

ILLUSTRATOR BARBARA JOHNSON-COLON

To order additional copies of this book, contact:
Xlibris
1-888-795-4274
www.Xlibris.com
Orders@Xlibris.com

Contents

This book is dedicated to my family…

my husband, Ed our three

children, Jessica, Jake and Jori and their

spouses, Pete and Jessica,

and to their dedication in raising

the grandchildren in the nurture

and admonition of the Lord.

I love you—Callie, Bryce, Maddie, Lynnzie,

Isaac, Aleigha, Amanda and Olivia

You fill my life with joy and

anticipation!

Sis

Just a little girl
Carried by her dreams
Sneaks into the closet
To dress up like a queen

The dress hung off my shoulders
And the skirt was way too long
But that did not matter
In my heart I had a song

No performance could begin
Without a stage on which to stand
So I took Daddy's dictionary
And struck up the magic band

My song wafted to the ceiling
Without rhythm without rhyme
And I bowed at their ovation
The pleasure was all mine

All done with my performance
I opened the closet door
And took off my sister's prom dress
Left it crumpled on the floor

Kneeling by my bedside
I asked the Lord for this
That I could be just like her
My dearest grown up sis

Grandma's Purse

When I was just a little girl
My Grandma had a purse
In it she kept life's necessities
But dinner must come first!

She also had lipstick
In the prettiest of pink
I colored most my face
And asked Grandma
What'd she think

She reached inside her purse
To get a handkerchief out
Spit on it to clean me
My nose my cheeks my mouth

Then I saw Grandma's brag book
And opened it to see
So many lovely photos
And they were all of me!

The Sparrow

Like a tree by the water
Rooted deep, you draw your strength
Pointing up you send the message
Love's strong arm is short no length

You've heard the laughter of children playing
You've known the verse that lovers shared
You've seen the funny three-legged races
And ushered up many mother's prayers

Like a tree planted by the water
Summer, winter, fall the same
Through tempest you are undaunted
Loved by this sparrow in the rain.

Summer Day

Swinging and swinging
On a warm summer day
Aleigha and I
Were off to play
Push me higher
You said right out loud
I want to taste
The cotton candy clouds
Hold on tight then
I'll see what I can do
A huff and puff
And over you flew
You reared back and giggled
As you leaned into the sky
And you were tickled
By belly butterflies
On the way to the car
You picked every flower for me
And I explained to the ranger
We thought they were free!
Aleigha you are so much fun
To spend the day with
Its time to go now
So give me a kiss.

Shoes

Dad, I remember trying to wear your shoes
When I was only two
With all my heart I wanted
To do things you could do
By age four you were the talk among my friends
I told them you could wrestle a bear
And you would always win
Little boys grow up so soon
And so quickly become men
But I could never fill your shoes
Now, or way back then
I miss you now because you've past
But I wondered if you could see
My little boy Bryce tried on my shoes
And wants to be like me!

The Shield

He dipped the arrow in the poison of doubt

Then carefully aimed and let go

Carried by the wind it pierced my heart

When the arrow left the bow

The Father prayed 'pick up your shield

Your faith it can protect'

But what will I do when the battle's too strong

And the enemy moves in for the kill?

"Your faith is enough because and beyond

I cover you with my will"

No fiery darts can get to you

If you don't let them in

So pick up your faith and carry on

The battle is within!

Mr. Nobody

Hey Bubba, what was that?

I don't know, go to sleep

Maybe it's the cat

I don't think so

Get down and go see

No way—oh no

But you can bunk with me

I'll bring you up your sword

But I'm gonna tell Mamma

There's a monster behind the door!

Give me your sword

And make the pillow case my cape

I've got to get to Mom

Before it is too late!

Down the creaky ladder

As fast as I could go

I stabbed the chair and garbage can

On the way to let Mom know

Mamma, Mamma there's

A monster in my room!

Isaac, you are mistaken

There is no pending doom.

Come with me

There's someone you must meet

I've known him since I was a girl

And he's really very sweet.

He comes at night most the time

To find long lost toys

Sometimes you'll hear a thump

But he doesn't mean to make noise

His name is Mr. Nobody

Let's see if he is here

No, not there, maybe the closet

I guess he's gone now, dear

He is very much in demand

So maybe he's next door

Now go to sleep Isaac

Don't be afraid anymore

Princess

When you opened your birthday gifts
Your face lit up so bright
As you saw the princess dress
With shoes and scepter that light

How fast you put them on
So everyone could see
That you were Princess Lynnzie now
And belonged in royalty

The grace with which you reigned
Was perfect for your age
All the cake you wanted
And no one else on stage

Your loyal subjects cheered you on
And each game let you win
Till the scepter dropped and tiara cocked
The Princess was done in

I cradled you in my arms
All done with all the games
I took you to your castle
The Princess that bears my name

The Dream

A sleepy haze
To start my day
My dream was hidden by the night

Whatever it was
It was precious because
Hope sprang up inside

Each time the dream
Would leave me something
Always a gift to my soul

Belonging or peace
It would release
But the dream I could not know

What is it I prayed
That is hidden away
Belonging only to me?

God lifted the disguise
When I looked in your eyes
I knew you were the man of my dreams

The Broken Angel

The Christmas tree stood trimmed and lit
And set the room aglow
The light danced across the room
And put on quite a show
It spoke such peace to all who looked
And seemed to draw me in
It promised gifts to each of us
Because of how we'd been
But then I saw the strangest thing
Right there and in full view
A beautiful, but broken angel
With wings broken in two
I thought that this must be wrong
So I asked my mom that night
To exchange the broken one
For one whose wings were right
She sat me down and spoke to me
In words I'll never shirk
She said that angel sang a special song
To tell to all the earth
That Jesus would come from heaven
To a lowly stable birth
But why did God use an angel
With a broken wing?
Because the angel's message
Was the most important thing
You mean Jesus saw the angel's heart
And not the angel's wing?
Why that's the kind of love that could make
Every angel sing
So I took the broken angel
And placed it at the top
And trumpeted the message
Newly written in my heart!

The Allegory

The howling winds bent the trees
The storm was on its way
Never sure of what's ahead
I looked for a place to stay
Panic seized my senses
As debris flew through the air
No hope for rescue
Because no one was there
Captured by the whirlwind
Entangled by my loss
I wondered if there was room
For this sinner at the cross
A mighty gust compelled me
And I blew right through a door
Just inside I laid there
A heap upon the floor
The silence was deafening
A sweet savor filled the air
I knew that I was not
The only person there
The air in that room
Had a healing balm
Just breathing in and out
Left me feeling calm
Where was I, I wondered
But I did not know
Stuttering I made requests
In a tone quiet and low
One right after another
Till I was inside out
My requests were made known
They were heard without a doubt
A newness was about me
So I got up to leave
Different than I came in
Because now I believed
Exiting the knobless door
I could read inscribed
"Ask, seek and knock
For the King lives inside"
Stepping back so I could read
The address of that place
I read to my amazement
It was the Throne Room of Grace

The Clothesline

The sun was straight up in the sky
And the wind blew my hair
Mom was hanging clothes
To dry in the noonday air

The socks were hung in perfect pairs
The sheets and then the shirts
My shadow was my playmate
We danced barefoot in the dirt

Sometimes the load was too heavy
And the clothesline would sag
Mom would prop a stick up
So the middle would not drag

When the sun came up this morning
The scent of sun-drenched sheets
Brought back those Kodak moments
My memory will always keep

And just like that sagging line
When my load was way too much
You came alongside and propped me up
With that look, a word or a touch

What a perfect picture the clothesline
Will always be
When Momma gave support
To a drooping saggy me.

Together

Before the sun sank one day
I saw the sweetest thing
An aged man walking with his wife
At dusk in early spring

They were not in much of a hurry
It seemed they had all day
His arm wrapped in hers
He helped steady their way

A closer look at their faces
Revealed their weathered brows
Time exchanged tribulation
For sweet contentment now

She gave to him the lunch she made
He gave to her his coat
Life's questions now had answers
And the trials seemed remote

Rising from their park side bench
They made their way toward home
Hand in hand they traveled
Thankfully not alone

That suspended moment
Made me wonder how it'd be
When all that we have left
Is only him and me

So I took my husbands arm
And held it closer in mine
Turned my collar to the wind
And learned to treasure time

Connectedness

The lighthouse stood as monument of strength
No tempest could aswage
I longed to find rest there
For at least a night and day.

At night we'd hear the lapping waves
Knocking at the eaves
A lullaby from God
Heard only by the sea.

Sleep would be the perfect time
To learn of sailor's lore
Suspended for that night
Between the earth and shore

Morning would have a gift
A gift for you and me
The gift of connectedness
Given only by the sea.

Panda Bear

Rigidy Gig
And away we go
We're going to see
Amanda's show
Popcorn and candy
When I came in
Oh what fun
Let the show begin
Three little bears
On their tippy-toes
Ballet for me
Well what do you know
One bear wore red
The other's pink and blue
They were so cute
In their little tutus
The bears did tricks
One by one
Bear hugs are soft
And so much fun
Dancing and dancing
Until morning came
Then I woke up
And called out your name
Grandma, grandma
Did you see the Pandas?
No, but you can tell me
All about it Amanda!

Good Counsel

No matter how many people are in the room
I'm the one you gravitate to
That's a gift from you to me
Thanks for what you do

You are not caged in by life's demands
You're always ready to go
You and me down the road
For a day, a week or so

No matter how intimate our talk is
You listen till I'm done
And I know you'd never tell a soul
No, not even one

You don't require fancy toys
The simple things are fine
You are not demanding at all
You are such a rare find

Every marriage could be greater
And their hopes not in a fog
If they'd learn these life lessons
That I learned from my own dog.

Wisdom

His eyes were soft
Concerned and muted blue
They were void of prejudice
And ambitious things to do

Each day he'd rock on the porch
Watching the world go by
Wisdom was muffled
By his quiet, helpless sigh

Experienced erased his ego
Left behind more noble cause
But shame left his wisdom his
Because no one stopped to pause

Like the snowdrift in winter
Is blown silently from here to there
He's forever gone now
And only the wind rocks the chair

Rain

Tear shaped pain
Fell like rain
When the news thunder-clapped my soul

I want to know why
And I only cry
As I reap what I have not sown

All the grieving
Is cured by believing
That You minister to each of Your own

The heavens seem locked
But I know they're not
I'll drift from this night to the morn

But please fix my pain
Give laughter in the rain
And the courage to embrace the storm

Night Over

Mom and Dad dropped me off
At my grandparents one day
A kiss, a hug "goodbye Madeline"
And Mom and Dad were on their way

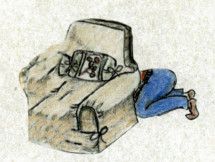

And Grandpa told funny stories
About Grandma's belly
And it shook when she laughed
Like a bowl full of jelly

We played hide and seek
And I'd always win
Because Grandma and Grandpa
Aren't very thin

Grandma and Grandpa were tired
So we all went to bed
They snored so loud
I put my pillow over my head

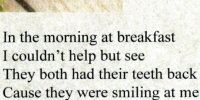

I had to go to the washroom
So tiptoeing pretty far
I found to my amazement
Grandpa's teeth were in a jar

In the morning at breakfast
I couldn't help but see
They both had their teeth back
Cause they were smiling at me

The Curious Two

It's a curious thing, the two of us
Curious indeed
How God could take two child-like hearts
And make them you and me

You did not know what lied ahead
When you said "I do"
You simply took my hand in yours
And off together we flew

Ups and downs have come and gone
Life's problems have been dealt
But never once in all these years
Have I questioned how you felt.

Don't ever stop being just who you are
And letting the Lord lead.
After all He's brought us this far
This couple called you and me!

Mommy's Helper

One day I did the funniest thing
To help Mommy out
I did all the laundry
She'd be happy no doubt

I put as many clothes in the washer
As I could possibly fit
And a bottle of laundry soap
To get clean as clean could get

I didn't forget the bleach
I had seen Mommy pour
Then I played in the bubbles
That went all over the floor

Finally the load was done
And I put it in to dry
But what I did not expect
Was such a fun surprise

Dad's drab white shirts
They came out pink
So much better than before
At least that's what I think

The blue jeans now had white spots
Too big to be missed
I don't know how it happened
I can't wait till Mom sees this

The dryer buzzed loudly
And down the stairs I flew
Brought up all the clothes
All looked somehow new

I could tell Mom was surprised
"Wow, thank you, Livy" she cheered
I couldn't help but notice
Mommy welled up in tears!